How to Make Money Fast!

Fast & Easy Ways to Make Extra Money

By

David Peters

Disclaimer

Everyone is different and every situation and location is different as well. Because of this it is not possible to give anyone a definitive way of accomplishing anything that will work 100% of the time. It is the responsibility of the reader to determine which parts of this publication, if any, are appropriate and effective for them at any given time and in any given situation. The writers, publishers and sellers assume no responsibility and express no guarantees of earnings or individual success.

Contents

Introduction

There will always be times in our lives when we could use or really need some extra money. Whether it be a few dollars to go out to eat of several hundred dollars to pay off some bills or meet an unexpected expense, the great news is that it can be fairly easy for most of us to make extra money when we need it.

Sometimes the need is temporary in the case of paying off an unexpected bill while other times we might find that we will need some extra money every month for the foreseeable future. Whatever your need might be we are here to show you how to meet it and hopefully exceed it. It just might be easier than you think!

Before we get started, let me say right from the start that the best time to make a little bit of extra money is before you actually need it. Don't wait for an unexpected expense to put pressure on you financially.

We almost always do a better job when we have the time to think things through and plan accordingly. When we are rushed or under pressure that is when we do things we might not ordinarily do.

This book is divided into 2 parts. The first part involves how to make the best decisions and how to choose the best options for you. This is really important because while we might need a few extra dollars we do not want to make our lives miserable in the process. Our goal should be to make the extra money and enjoy ourselves in the process.

The second part of the book will give you some ideas on how you can go about making some extra money. Though not every idea will appeal to you or even be appropriate, you will find a few things that will appeal to you. Just pick one or two and take some action.

By using the first and second parts of this book together, you will find yourself making the money you need with the least negative impact on your lifestyle. After all, while having extra money is nice, it is not the most important thing in life. So read the first part of the book and take action with the second part. Together you will find yourself with a few extra bucks in your wallet and a smile on your face.

Goals

As strange as it might seem, we need to get an idea of what kind of money we need to make before we get started. The actual amount of money is usually going to be a mixture of desires and reality. For example, all would love to make $1,000,000 in the next 6 months but reality often dictates something else entirely.

It is a good idea to understand what we need so we can make the right decisions moving forward. For example, if we just need $75 to pay for a new battery for our car, then we might be able to sell a few things on EBAY or do a small task for someone in order to get that much money.

But if we need $500 to pay for a major repair or other expense, then we probably would have to do something different because earning $500 is more difficult than earning $75.

Because of this our decisions and options are going to be different and we want to make the best choice so we can hit our goal and get what we need.

I usually like to aim on the high side because rarely do people complain about having an extra $100 in their wallet but most people would be upset if they came up short of what they really need when they needed it. So a little bit of planning now will help us greatly in the future.

Time frame is important as well because most of the time when we need extra money we need it within a specific time frame or it will cost us even more money. For example, if you need $500 by the end of the month and you only make $300 by that time then you will be $200 short and that would probably result in finance charges and even more debt.

That is why we have said earlier that the best time to plan on making extra money is before you need it. This way we can work out a few longer range plans that will have a much more favorable result for us. The more option we have the more likely we will find one that will give us the best result with the fewest negatives or complications.

For example, if you know you will need $500 in 3 months, you can earn a little bit a week over the next 12 weeks and you will have what you need. You can create a plan and work towards it. Maybe your plan would be to create an item and sell it to people at a craft fair or at work or even on-line. That could be a legitimate option for a 3 month time frame.

But if you needed $500 by the end of the week that might require you to sell a few of your things that you might otherwise prefer not to sell or take out a loan and pay finance charges or interest on the money that you borrowed. Both of those options are far from optimal but might be necessities based on such a short time frame. So planning ahead definitely has its positive side.

For this reason I would plan on making a bit more than you need so that you can start an emergency fund that will enable you to meet unexpected expenses without having to react to those last minute situations. When you have such a fund you can draw from it as you need it and replace what you took out over time.

Long or Short Term

One last factor to consider is whether you are going to need this money for a short period of time or a long period of time. In other words, is your need for money right now the result of an unexpected expense or are you constantly falling short at the end of the month or right before payday? This is important because these are two different types of needs and we usually will need to address each of those needs differently.

Short-term needs can usually be addressed by taking a temp job or selling a few things to bring in the extra money. Examples of a short-term need might be to carry you over until your next paycheck or to give you funds during a temporary loss of employment. In other words, a temporary need is to get you through a situation that is out of the ordinary.

Long-term needs are another matter. If you are constantly falling behind every month and always need another $100 or $200 to get you through the month, then selling a couple of things is not a viable option as eventually you will run out of things to sell.

Borrowing money definitely is not an option either as the costs of interest will just make it harder and more impossible to pay your bills next month. The result is that you will have to borrow even more next month and the month after that and so on.

If we have a short-term need we can address that with one-shot actions like selling things or doing something one or two times to get you what you need. These are the easiest situations to address. They require short-term efforts and sacrifice which most people are willing to do.

Long-term needs often require a change in lifestyle or employment. In other words you are either going to have to change your lifestyle to reduce expenses or change your employment situation so that you are bringing in more money every month. The bottom line here is that you either have to earn more or spend less in order to make it through every month.

So try and determine what you need and for how long you are going to need it for. That will help you determine what you need to do to resolve your problems both now and moving forward. Evaluate your financial situation and be honest with yourself. Don't try and convince yourself that things are better than they really are. If you try and do that you will just make things   worse   over   time.

Likes & Dislikes

In the second part of this book you are going to find a list of ideas and things you can do to bring in a bit of extra money when you need it. Some of these things will appeal to you and some you might find a bit repulsive. After all each of us is different and each of us has things that we like to do and things we try to avoid at all costs.

When it comes to money, we usually have to do something to get it. We cannot just pick it off of a magic money tree or expect others to just give us what we need when we need it. So since we have to do something to get the money we need we might as well do something we enjoy or at least find tolerable.

I think it is a great idea to make a list of all the things you like to do and another list of the things we just cannot stand doing. Don't hold back and be perfectly honest with yourself. Don't let money factor into your decision at least at this time. If you try and convince yourself that something you hate isn't so bad you might make the wrong decision later on.

Here is something most people don't realize when it comes to money. Money at best is a temporary motivator. By that I mean that it makes you happy for a limited amount of the time and once that period of time passes the reality comes back.

For example, if you hate your job but the boss gives you a big raise you might be happy for a few paychecks. But then you get used to the money and the same things that caused you to hate your job before are still there and you will start hating your job again. So unless you get another big raise you are not going to be happy.

When we decide how we are going to earn our money we need to take two things into consideration. We should try to earn our money doing something we like or enjoy and we should choose something that will address the reality of the situation. In other words, we want to do something we like that will enable us to make the money we need when we need it.

The exception to this might be a limited time or one-shot action that will resolve your financial problem. Most of us can do something we don't enjoy if we just have to do it once or twice and then walk away from it. Most of us would work long hours for a while to build a strong business that will help us in the future. We wouldn't want to work those hours for years and years but for a short-term we can see the benefit for working those hours.

As I said we are all different and there are people who making their living cleaning up dog poor for people and are doing quite well and they enjoy being outside and doing that job. Other might be repulsed by that and might prefer writing a resume for other people or building crafts in their basement.

There is no one perfect answer to how you should go about making your money. But you should try and pick something you can enjoy so that you will have a good time making your money. After all, if it is not considered work you would be far more likely to stick with it longer and get a greater benefit from whatever it is that you are doing.

This is even more important when it comes to resolving a long-term financial need where whatever you decide to do will become part of your lifer for the foreseeable future. The longer you are going to need to do something the more important it is that you should like it. Because once the novelty of the money wears off you are going to be miserable doing something you hate.

Problems & Solutions

Here is a concept so very basic and easy it is shocking to see how many people fail to understand it and act upon it. If you can just embrace this one simple philosophy you will find it much easier to identify opportunities in life that just might be staring you right in the face!

This one simple concept is as follow:

Everything we do to earn money in life either involves solving a problem or being part of the solution.

Just think about that for a moment. Every job we do either resolves a problem or involves us being part of a solution. From the CEO of a company down to the person who cleans out the restrooms, everything we do at our jobs either solves a problem or is part of that solution.

Every product we buy we buy because it either solves a problem or makes something faster or easier.

The detergent we use it bought because it solves the problem of how to get our clothes clean. At work the person who cleans out the restrooms does that because they need to be clean and sanitary. The cashier is there because someone has to take money and process sales. The salesman is there to answer questions and help generate sales. If the products sold themselves we would have no need to hire salespeople.

So when it comes to making money, ask yourself which problems are you best able to solve? Ask yourself how you can be part of a solution to a problem? Then take your skills and abilities and match them to those problems or solutions and see what you have to offer. There is something that everyone can do when they look hard enough.

The person with the two story house and who is afraid of heights is looking for someone to clean his gutters. Could you be that person? If you enjoy being outside and do not have a fear of heights that could represent a real opportunity for you.

The person who works 80 hours a week might not look forward to spending their Saturday's mowing the lawn or cleaning their house. Could those be opportunities for you as well? Look for problems that you can solve and you will come up with a laundry list of opportunities that you can take advantage of and earn some extra money.

The same goes for products you might design or produce. If you make something that makes a common task easier or faster, you will probably be able to find a market for it. All you have to do is match a problem or a need with the right product and you might have all the money you need!

Don't waste time trying to do something that no one has a need for. There are too many real needs that are going unaddressed to keep you busy for a long time. Just find one that appeals to you and your skills and you will be well on your way!

Do What is Necessary

Pay close attention to this chapter because, like the last chapter, it represents a unique outlook on how you can make as much money as you want no matter where you live or what you are capable of doing.

Many people became successful by following one simple outlook on life. That outlook is that they would be willing to do things that other people were not willing to do. These are the tasks or chores that some people feel are "beneath them" or that they are just too good for. These are often the markets that are either untapped or under-utilized. Therefore they can represent gold mines of opportunity for those who recognize them and are willing to do what it takes to be successful in those markets.

As you take a look at the opportunities that are around you, don't think that you are better than anyone else or that anything is beneath you. People have made massive amounts of money just because they were willing to do what someone else wasn't. There are many examples of this in every town and neighborhood.

Take a look at the advertisements you see in your town. You will see advertisements for people to come and clean up your dog poop or for people to go up and clean the gunk out of your gutters. There are services that will come and pump out your cesspool or septic tank. People who will come and clean your house or walk your dog.

None of those examples are things anyone should be ashamed of. Every one of those examples solves a problems that many of us have in life. Every one of the people who perform those services or works in those jobs should be proud of what they do. Not because they are glamorous careers or jobs but because they are being productive and helping make other people's life better.

Don't be afraid to take on a task that others refuse to take on. Instead be proud that you are taking advantage of a legitimate opportunity. You don't have to do certain things forever but sometimes you might have to do something early on in order to move on to bigger and better things.

Don't let pride get in the way of you achieving your dreams. Do what you need to do, as long as it is legal, in order to get what you want in life. You owe it to yourself to do what needs to be done, no matter what that might be.

Fast vs. Slow

It should come as no surprise to you that some forms of earning or making money take longer than others. While that does not mean they are wrong choices or not the best choices, they will have some impact on what is the best for you.

If you need money now, like in today or tomorrow, you are almost going to have to do something very locally such as mow a lawn, paint a room or do something for a friend or neighbor. These are the things that will get you money right away. You might also sell something to a friend, visit the local pawn shop or sell things in a yard or garage sale.

All of those choices will get you money immediately and will allow you to have what you need when you need it. However there are other ways of making money that might take a while for you to get paid. These might be a good choice for getting money in a week or a month or to fund a recurring need for money but will not help you get money by tonight.

Getting a part-time job, for example will usually require you to wait a week or more for the hours you worked today. But those jobs will continue to earn you money as long as you work so in exchange for a bit of a wait you will have more money over a long period of time. It's a trade-off and one that might be well worth it to you.

So when you are deciding on what to do to get a little more money coming in, always ask yourself when you really need that money because some choices are not going to get you what you need while others will. You just need to know up-front so that you can make the best decisions.

One-Shot vs. Recurring

Here is one more thing to think about when it comes to earning or making money. Some of the things you can do will being you in money when you need it. Examples of this might be selling something, mowing a lawn or completing a similar task or taking any form of action that will result in a one-time infusion of cash.

These are called one-shot efforts and they provide a result whenever you do them. You choose what to do, you earn the money and you move on. The next time you need money you choose something else to do and the process starts all over again.

That is good when you need money on a periodic or infrequent basis but also has the disadvantage of having to start all over again from square one whenever you need money. But there are other ways to bring money in that require you to do something once and those efforts continue to bring in money over and over again.

That is called recurring revenue and it can be a great option for you if you are able to generate this type of revenue. Examples of recurring revenue might be writing a book. You write it once and every time you sell a copy you earn some money from the sale. Another example would be starting a business. You go through all the steps once and then every time you make a sale you make money.

Let's say you have a lot of recipes that you really like and think that others would enjoy. So you put them all together, create a website for them and put them on sale on the internet. You do all that work one time and then let it make you money time and time again in the future. People do this all the time. Any time where you do something once and it keeps producing for you is called recurring revenue and it can be a powerful income generating tool for you.

The approach that I suggest, even when you need money right away, is to take care of your immediate needs first by doing something that will get you money NOW but then also putting things in motion to create some recurring revenue in the future as well. I suggest this because if something happened to you now that caused you to need money quickly chances are it is going to happen to you again in the future as well. So why not take action now to prepare yourself for later?

The best approach to making more money is to address both long-term and short-term needs at the same time. No one has lost sleep over having too much money and no one has ever regretted becoming more prepared and secure in the future either. Besides when we set up sources of recurring revenue now, we can do so at our leisure where we have more control over the process and far less stress.

The other great thing about recurring revenue is that you do not have to create something that brings in thousands every month although you can certainly do that. But even if you just generate an extra $50 a month from something, once you find something that works you can duplicate it over and over and over again! Imagine having 10 sources that each bring in $50 a month! That is $500 each and every month without much effort on your part!

Creating recurring revenue takes work and the first time you try it you will probably spend more time doing it. But as you get used to the process and discover shortcuts and easier ways of accomplishing the same results, the entire process will get easier and faster.

If you want to get to financial freedom faster and easier than most people, use a two pronged approach of both one-shot and recurring revenue to reach your goals. Eventually you will get to the point where you will no longer require the one-shot efforts because your recurring revenue will meet all your financial requirements and then some.

Earning More in Your Career

Any book on how to make more money would be remiss if we didn't even touch on one of the best ways to earn more money and that is through getting more money in your current job or by finding a better one. Let's face it, we need more money because what we are earning in our current job is not meeting our needs. When that happens we either have to adjust our needs or earn more money.

In order to earn more money you have to show yourself as being worthy of that money by increasing your value to the company in the eyes of your bosses and management. In other words, you have to show the people above you that you are worth more to the company than you are getting paid.

There is a misconception in this country today that people deserve raises and certain levels of compensation. While that is a nice thought to have it is so far from reality that it is not even close. You are worth exactly what your worth to the company is established to be. If your production is worth $50,000 a year you should not expect to be paid $75,000. That is just not reasonable. Your company should be able to take your contribution and make a profit on you. After all the entire focus of the company is to make profits. They cannot make profits if they pay you more than you are worth.

Need is also not a valid reason for a raise. If you need more money to live then you either need to show that you are worth it or increase your value in the marketplace. Get more education, get more experience or learn a new skills. In other words, find out what employers are looking for and find a way to get it and give it to them.

Improving yourself is the ultimate kind of recurring revenue. Every time you get a raise more money will be coming in with every paycheck. Every raise you get moving forward will be on top of the raise you just received. This is how people wind up with the huge salaries they make. They don't go from mail room clerk to CEO in one jump. They work at it.

The other thing you need to do is a bit of self-promotion. By that I mean put yourself out there so you get noticed. Volunteer for more projects, take the initiative and take on more responsibilities. Show people what you can do and show them that you are worth more to the company than what you are being paid.

This is how people are chosen for promotions. Good things happen to those who pursue them. Make it difficult for people to pass you by for a promotion. Get yourself noticed and good things will happen. But if they don't for some reason, there are other alternatives that you need to explore as well.

One of the best ways to increase your salary at a faster rate is by changing companies that you work for. You will usually earn larger increases by changing companies than you would if you got a promotion in your current job. Of course money isn't everything and you should not get a reputation as a job hopper either but moving around from time to time will help you earn more money earlier in your career.

But always keep in mind that you are worth what your skills, talents and abilities are worth in the marketplace. Do not think or feel that you are worth more simply because you have been with the company for a number of years. You should be compensated based on your overall worth not just because of how long you sat behind that desk. You need to keep your skills fresh, sharp and current in order to enhance your value to others.

One last thing. Avoid the "entitlement virus" at all costs. Do not think you are owed anything in life. If you want something, be willing to work for it. Do not expect it to be handed to you.

You will find that the more you work for the things you want in life the more will be handed to you based on those efforts.

People want people who are not afraid to work for what they want. What they don't want are people who sit back and demand that everything be given to them.

So if you want something in your job whether it be more money in your paycheck or a promotion or other benefit, find out what you need to get there and then start working at it. When you start working for what you want, good things will happen.

Create Boundaries
& Balance

Before we get started on giving you some fresh and innovative ideas, we would be remiss if we did not insert a bit of balance and perspective at this point in the book. While we need money to survive and live in this world, money should not be the primary driving force behind everything that we do. We should do our best to create a balanced life where we give our attention and efforts into everything that is important and not just money.

We often focus so much on money and careers that we lose sight of other things in our lives that just might be more important to our overall happiness. Our family, friends and relationships are where the real joy and fulfillment in life come into play. We must not move those things to the side and concentrate on just money.

We should also mention that there are two ways to have more money in our lives. We can either earn more money or spend less. The end result is the same. We either make more money or get more out of the money we currently have. The choice is yours.

They say that money cannot buy happiness and that is most certainly true. But the real truth is that the people who say that are usually the people that have the most money for whatever reason. These people understand that money cannot buy everything in life. But even those people understand that money does play an important role in our lifestyle and overall comfort.

What we need to have in our lives is a balance between what is really important in life and what we need to survive. No one wants to go through life with the bare minimum but we also do not need gross excess either. What we need is something right in the middle where we have enough to live well without abandoning or setting aside other parts of our lives.

It is perfectly normal and natural to want the better things in life. But do not allow money to be the driving force between everything that you do and say in life. In other words, do not allow money to control and rule over your life. Create both financial and emotional balance so that you can lead an emotionally fulfilling life.

If you can manage this in your life you will find yourself being happier and living under much less stress. Money will give you options. Just use those options to lead the life you really want not the life money forces you to lead.

Part Two:

26 Ways to Get
Money Fast!

Mow Lawns

From our teenage years to well into adulthood mowing a lawn or providing landscape services is one way of earning money in your spare time. If you enjoy this sort of thing there is no limit on the amount of money you can make. In fact, this is one of the most common ways people earn extra money.

It is a cash business where you usually get paid on the spot so when you need money quickly this can be the ideal option for you. If there is grass in your neighborhood, there are opportunities for you. There are a lot of people who dislike mowing their lawns or just don't have the time to do it themselves and they will be happy to pay someone to do it for them.

Offer Painting Services

A LOT of people hate painting their houses both on the interior and exterior. They hate the mess, going on ladders and all the hard work that goes with doing a good job. In fact, many people do not know how to get a really professional result or the proper way of applying paint so that it will last.

If you have the expertise to do a good job and are willing to do that at a fair price you can wind up not only with a nice amount of money in your pocket but a host of recommendations as well.

Be sure to have the required licenses that may be required in your area.

Clean Pools

If you live in an area where people have pools there is always a demand for people to come in every week and clean those pools, add chemicals and maintain the filters and other equipment. You can also offer pool opening and closing services as well.

You can do the same with lawn sprinkler systems as well. Most people have little or no idea on how to properly maintain or winterize their sprinkler systems.

Be sure to comply with any local licensing laws that may be in effect.

Clean Houses

There are a lot of people who either do not like to clean their own homes or just do not have the time to do so. With more and more households needing both people working, time is at a premium for these families. The last thing they want to do is work hard all week and then have to clean their house on their days off!

This is where you come in. You offer cleaning services to those people who would rather pay someone else to clean their homes instead of them doing it themselves. As we said, where there is a problem you can be the solution!

Organize Houses

If you have the skills and know-how, there is a huge demand for people to come in and organize a home. That means getting rid of clutter, organizing possessions and making it easier to find things and make the home nicer and easier to live in.

This can also include the sales and installation of closet organizers and other supplies and products. Since you can charge a mark-up on all of these products you can even make more money on every job!

Scoop Poop!

OK, this one might be a bit gross but that is exactly why there is a high demand for these services. Any home who has a pet is a potential client for a waste removal service. You just come a couple of times a week, gather up the pet waste and dispose of it.

Yeah, it's a crappy job but you can also earn a crap-load of money doing it! (Sorry, couldn't resist!)

Clean Out Gutters

There are millions of people like me that hate going up on tall ladders and cleaning out of the leaves and wet gunk that clogs their gutters. But just because we hate doing it doesn't mean it doesn't have to get done.

Clogged getters can result in water entering behind the gutters and destroying the structure of the home. So like it or not, gutters need to be cleaned.

You can offer the service to all your fellow homeowners and do it with a minimal investment. You will need a few ladders. A couple of buckets and some gloves. You can even offer installation of gutter covers and other products at the same time. This is a service that will give you recurring revenue every year as long as your prices are appropriate and your service good.

Sell a Product or Craft

If you have a hobby or do a craft that you can sell, this can be a gold mine for you. Sell at craft fairs, school events and local venues. Sell online or in magazines as well. You can even hold craft workshops where you teach others and provide materials to your students.

There are endless opportunities for those who have a skills that is demand by others. Your only limitation is your imagination and your particular skill. Sell products, give classes, teach others or create social events and home sales!

Baby or Adult Sit

Every area have families that either have small children or older adults that require supervision at some times of the day.

Baby-sitting used to be very common but now providing companionship to older adults is also commonplace as well.

If you have the personality that lends itself to this kind of job then you can earn a decent income in the evenings or on weekends. This can make it easy to hold down a full time job and work on this after hours.

Just understand that this kind of work requires patience and understand as well as a lot of compassion. There is also a great deal of responsibility required as well. Depending on the services you provide there might be licensing requirements as well.

House Sit

It has been said that an empty house is an open invitation for thieves to come in and take everything that you own. To help prevent this a lot of people opt to pay someone to come in and live in their home while they are away. That gives the home the appearance of being lived in and that alone will scare thieves away.

Keep in mind that you will probably have to be bonded so that the homeowners will be protected against you stealing or damaging their home. References are going to be required as well so it might be difficult to get your first few jobs until you can build up some references.

Save or Turn in Loose Change

A few years ago I started throwing my change into a large jug in the corner of my bedroom. Last year I wanted to buy an expensive camera to start learning photography. The camera was going to set me back over $1,000 so I thought I would get maybe a few hundred from emptying my change jug.

I emptied it and to my surprise I found I had over $1,300 in that jug. All from a few pennies a day left over in my pants pocket! This was a nice little windfall. Just choose a jug or container that is not easy to open and dip into and you will find yourself with a nice little nest egg when you need it!

Sell Things

We all have things in our homes that we never use anymore or have become outdated. The great thing is that these things that have little value to us might have considerable value to someone else! Sell these things to local consignment shops or antique shops to get a quick infusion of extra cash.

For those who don't need the money this minute you can sell anything on sites like e-bay and other online selling sites. Then the money is sent to PayPal where you can either buy other stuff or transfer it to your bank account. In some cases you can have spendable cash in your hands within a few days to a week!

Return Purchases You Don't Use

OK, I used to work in retail and I used to hate the people who would come in and ask for refunds on stuff they bought over a year ago. But the fact remains that if you have receipts and unopened products that were given to you as gifts or that you no longer want or need, you might be able to return those items for a refund of store credit.

Just check the return policies and make sure what you are returning is complete and in good condition. In other words, be responsible and try not to unload crap another unsuspecting customer will end up buying and taking home only to find it doesn't work.

Recycle Metal or Other Items

Metal items, especially copper and other metals, have recycling value. It might be possible for you to take those few old metal outdoor chairs you don't want and get cash for the metal in them. Junkyards pay cash based on weight so why not give it a try. You will get rid of some old junk and make a few dollars at the same time.

But be careful as some metals and items might be worth a lot more than you could get at a scrap yard. Evaluate every item before you decide where you would get the most money for your items.

Sell Jewelry

This is one of those items that you should not go to a junk yard! Gold, platinum and silver can pay you a lot of money if you take it to the right jeweler. It is not unusual to get several hundred dollars for some items. So if you have unwanted jewelry or items that have gone way out of style, this could be an easy way for you to get a lot of money almost instantly.

But please be careful because there are a lot of scammers out there who will either pay you less than you deserve or not pay you at all. Go to a reputable jeweler that you trust. Be especially careful with mail order or internet companies as once you send your items away you lose control over what happens to them. When you deal in person you can just walk away if you don't get what you feel is a fair deal. When you mail items away, you have little control after they are gone.

Rent out Space

If you have a large garage or basement consider renting out that space to people who have items that they would like to store somewhere. Just be careful about what you allow in your home or storage location. You want to stay away from hazardous materials, stolen items or other things that could cause you trouble.

Also be advised that you should be insured against theft and damage for everything that is stored on your premises.

Not everyone's insurance will cover items stored that belong to others. There also might be licensing or permitting issues involved as well so be sure to check that out as well.

Sell Online

There are several on-line sites that enable you to list various items you would like to sell to others. If you have old items that you no longer want consider selling them. You might not think something has much value but you never know until you try. Your junk might be someone else's gold mine!

If you are mechanically minded you might consider taking apart devices like appliances and vehicles and selling the individual parts. In some cases you can get several times more for the individual parts than you could for the entire product! But it takes time and space to do all of that. But if this interests you it could be a great way to earn extra cash.

Hold a Yard or Garage Sale

Everyone has seen and visited yard sales and many of us have held one or two as well. This is a great way to get money right away as all yard sales involved strictly cash purchases. But also consider that people are always looking for something for nothing so be prepared to accept low prices for your items and to constantly negotiate.

Some areas now require permits so investigate that. Also, do not let people into your home to look at what you have for sale. Keep everything outside so people do not have to enter your home. Do not let strangers use the bathroom either. This is because some people use this opportunity to see what's inside your home to see if it is worthwhile to come back later and rob you. This is sad but true.

Fix Things

Over the years I have made tens of thousands of dollars fixing things for people. I enjoyed the work, it paid me very well and I had a lot of fun in the process. By best day was when I worked for a little more than 2 hours and made over $500!

Just put a few advertisements out there or tell friends and associates about the services you offer. As you do work for more and more people your word of mouth advertising from satisfied customers will keep you in business!

Sign up for a Trial Study

Though this is not for everybody, there are various medical and psychological studies that will pay you a fee for participating. If you will receive some other benefits such as relief from a disease or other medical condition, this might be worthwhile for you.

But be careful and thoroughly understand what is involved before signing up. If it is a medical study be sure to consult with your family doctor as well.

Sell Bodily Fluids

This is something else that certainly isn't for everyone either. In some areas it is legal to sell blood or other bodily fluids such as semen. As I said it is not for everyone but it is one way you can make a few dollars almost immediately.

Take in a Roommate or Border

We talked about renting space and another option might be to rent out a room in your house or apartment to someone looking for a place to live. This is good because it provides recurring revenue every month or week depending on how they pay you.

But you should also be cautious because allowing someone into your home also means giving them access to you and everything that you own. For this reason it is best to rent only to people you know or who were recommended by people you trust. Even in those situations you can never be 100% certain so there is some risk involved. Also check out your insurance to see if renter's property is covered or how it might impact your other coverage.

Pawn Things

Pawn shops have been around for ages and they are one source for instant cash. You can either sell things direct to them or take out a short-term loan by leaving your property with them as collateral. But be careful because the interest rates are extremely high as compared to other loans. But they do pay immediately and this could be the right option for you.

Scavenge

This might or might not be for you but we have all seen the people who go around on garbage day picking things out of the trash. If you recycle metal garbage day can get you several hundred pounds of metal you can sell.

Or maybe you might see a piece of furniture that you could pick up and repair or refinish and use it or sell it. Even going through cans on recycling day and picking out deposit bottles can get you a decent payday when you redeem them. It is tedious and difficult work, and sometimes embarrassing but if you need money bad enough, it is an option.

Sell Your Opinions

There are a lot of place, mostly on-line, where you can fill out surveys or be part of an opinion poll. You get a fee for each poll or survey you fill out.

But there are also a lot of rip-offs out there as well so if any company wants to charge you a fee to join their organization before they give you surveys to fill out, look somewhere else. Also do not fall for claims that you can earn thousands of dollars a month either. That is a red flag when it comes to rip-offs and scammers.

Be a Temp Worker

Some people love being a temp worker because they can work when they want or as much or little as they want and they also get to do different jobs all the time. Temp workers, depending on their skill sets can earn a nice income working on a day to day basis.

You usually have to sign up for a tem agency but sometimes companies have their own internal temp program so look for advertisements and notices to see if any companies in your area offer this type of arrangement.

Become an Internet Affiliate

This is one of those opportunities that you have to be careful with. There are a lot of people who make a great deal of money selling affiliate products on-line. But this is not as easy as it might seem and it takes a while to build up a list of people likely to respond to your affiliate offers.

But there is an opportunity to build a really profitable business selling other people's products. When you do this you do not have to develop your own products, create websites or deliver the products yourself. You just get a commission for selling and the product owner does all the rest.

There are several companies that provide people with affiliate offers. A few of these are JVZOO, Clickbank, Commission Junction and MAX BOUNTY. None of these require a fee to join but as we said, it does take time to develop a list and make sales. Commissions are paid either directly or at the end of the month.

Offer On-Line Services

The internet can be a great way to earn extra money because it is so cheap to get started. You can get a domain for less than $15 and hosting for less than $5 a month. That is nothing compared to the cost of opening a brick and mortar store. So if you have products that you think will sell, or if you know someone who develops these types of products, this might be a great way to develop a steady stream of recurring revenue.

Last Resort Options

While money is important and sometimes critical to our living, there are sometimes limitations on what we should do as far as money is concerned. Whenever we need extra money we should make every effort to get that money in a positive manner that will not affect us negatively moving forward.

That means staying away from taking any action today that will result in making life more difficult tomorrow. Here are a few things we should think about avoiding or doing only as a last resort:

Take out a Short-Term Loan

Sometimes taking out a loan is the best answer especially when we have to make a required purchase that is very costly. An example of this might be a car loan. We all need transportation unless we live in an area covered well by mass transit. Very few people have $20,000 available in cash for a car. So they resort to taking out a loan.

The problem with loans is that it makes it much easier for us to purchase things we cannot afford or sometimes don't even need. Just because the opportunity is there does not mean that we should take advantage of it. We need to think twice, sometimes three times, before taking out a loan.

For example, if you need to replace your car, you do not have to get a new one if you cannot afford it. Get a good quality used car that will get you where you need to go in a reliable and safe manner. This can save you a ton of money while accomplishing the same goal.

But the really bad thing about loans is that the money you need today will have to be paid back, plus interest, in the months ahead. So if you are just making ends meet now and have to take out a loan that will make paying all your bills in the months ahead much harder if not impossible.

So make sure that you can afford the payments before taking out the loan. Check out interest rates and go with the lowest rate you can find. After all every dollar you pay in interest is one less dollar you will have to purchasing what you need in the future. You want to save as much of your money as you can for use by yourself not for others.

Think twice about whether you really need what you are thinking about taking the loan out for. Do you need it right now or can you wait and save up for it?

Is it absolutely essential or are there ways to do without it? In other words, be responsible with your finances and do not take out loans for things you really do not need.

We will get to this shortly but whatever you do, do NOT take out a cash advance loan on your credit cards because you will be paying a huge amount of interest that will force you deeper in debt.

Tap into Insurance or Retirement Funds

A lot of people will take loans out against their retirement or even take out funds to help them through tough times. While there may be legitimate reasons for doing this, it places not only your future retirement in jeopardy but also your ability to live life on your own terms.

In addition there are usually penalties for taking out finds before a certain age. So not only do you lose the interest on the money but you are paying penalties of 10% or more on whatever you remove. So if you need $10,000 you might have to withdraw $15,000 so you can pay the fees, penalties and taxes and still have that $10,000 left over.

Doing this may appear easy because there are no payments that have to be made next month or the months after. So this might be seen as a "pain-free" type of resolution. But the pain really comes later when you don't have enough money to retire and you find yourself having to work longer or living a very limited existence in retirement.

Sometimes this is a last resort when you are faced with losing your home to foreclosure or some other serious situation. In those cases seek counsel of a financial advisor who can advise you on what to do. Perhaps they can come up with other options that are less damaging to your future.

Credit Cards

Credit cards are one of the most convenient ways to spend money these days. In many cases, like renting a car, they are required for identification. But the sheer ease of using them, and the ability to charge more than you have in your savings can get people into deep trouble really quickly and easily.

The first thing to remember is that you should NEVER carry a monthly balance and pay interest charges. The interest on credit cards can reach as high as 27%!!!! That means you will wind up paying 27% higher prices on everything your purchase on your credit card when you carry a balance!

Most people do not realize that when you carry a balance that EVERY PURCHASE you make gets charged interest from the day you make the purchase. No 30 day grace period like people who pay in full every month enjoy! This can wind up costing you thousands of dollars in finance charges every year.

That is money that could have been used purchasing food, clothing and other items you need to survive.

Do not think that all you have to pay is the monthly minimum charges either. Those are designed to get you to pay more finance charges and earn the credit card companies even more money! You need to pay off those monthly balances in full or at least in the shortest time possible.

The best way to use credit cards is to buy only what you can afford to pay for that month. Use the convenience and the grace period to help you manage your finances but do not pay those crushing finance charges. In other words, do not spend money you don't have just because you can. That is precisely what the credit card companies want you to do. That is how they make their money.

Ways to Save Money!

Try and look at money this way: If you spend less, it is the same as having more. If you earn $2,000 a week and spend $2,000 a week, you are just keeping yourself financially afloat. But if you earn $2,000 a week and spend just $1,500 a week, that is the same as earning an extra $500! Either way you will have $500 left over at the end of the month. If you spend more than you earn, then reducing those expenses is even more important!

But the key to reducing expenses is to do so without a lot of sacrifice and inconvenience. This is important because the more we have to sacrifice or the worse it makes our lives the more likely it is that we will not keep doing what we need to do. So the smart way is to find easy and convenient ways to save money and get the most out of every dollar we make.

Here are a few things you can do to get more out of the money you already have or will make in the future:

Plan Accordingly

The best way to determine financial needs and money requirements and to get more out of the money you already have is to plan whatever expenses and purchases that you can. While there will always be unexpected expenses and while there is nothing you can do to forecast those expenses, you can forecast many of your most common expenses and plan for them.

Forecasting and planning expenses allows you to make more purchases when you have the money required to do so. This might mean postponing some purchases for a month or two or even realizing that some purchases should not be made at all at this time. This is all part of being financially responsible.

Proper planning will cut down on the need for loans and finance charges or interest. This will help you have more money available in the future which will enable you to get more out of the money you already have.

Create an Emergency Fund

Ideally we all would have a "slush fund" or emergency fund where we would have money for those unexpected expenses when they pop-up. But for some of us, extra money is just not a luxury or reality so we have to plan accordingly.

The best way to create this emergency fund is to put a couple of dollars a week or month and build the balance4 of the account over time.

If you need money right now, try and make a bit more than you need to get your account started. For example, if you need an extra $50 right now then put something in place that will bring in $75 and save that other $25.

Once you have started the account, do not touch it except in emergencies. Just because you have money in the account does not mean you can or should take it out to go out to dinner or take a vacation. Your emergency account should be for just that. Emergencies. This is part of being financially responsible.

Consolidate Loans

Some of us already have debt carried over from our past. This might be credit card debt, student loans, auto loans and other kinds of debt. Debt involves interest and interest is something that we use our money for without getting something in return. It is like throwing money away of lighting a fire with it.

Not all loans are the same and every loan has its own interest rates. The higher the rate the more interest you will pay so it makes sense to pay off those high interest loans first or sometimes even combining several high interest loans into one lower interest loan. The result is saving money on interest which will allow you to pay off the loans faster and with less cost.

Lower your Cable and Cell Phone Bills

Sometimes there are changes we can make that will help us save money without causing much impact, if any. Two of those expenses are our phone and cable or satellite TV bills. Do you really need all of those 457 channels in the master package or could you do without a few of them and save $20 a month? Do you really need satellite radio in your car or could you listen to "free" radio and save $150 a year?

Do you need all those minutes and data on your cell phone plan or could that be reduced as well? Are there specials or new customer discounts with other carriers available to you? Sometimes just switching carriers and keeping the same plans can save you a ton of money every year.

Most of us would be pleasantly surprised when we see how much money we could save with just a few minor changes we might not even feel at all!

Lower Insurance Costs

Everyone should re-evaluate their insurance coverage and costs at least once a year. Check what you pay against other companies to see if there are changes that should be made. Check your coverage to make sure that you have enough coverage and not too much. Things change over the year and we should not be over or under insured.

Cut or Eliminate Non-Essentials

Most of us pay for a lot of stuff that we really don't need or even use any longer. Maybe we don't use that boat anymore now that the kids are bigger. Maybe the huge house we once needed when we had our 5 kids living with us is too big now that they are all married or moved out.

Over our lifetimes we change and as we change so do our needs. We stop using something while we start using other things. But sometimes we still continue to pay for stuff we don't need or no longer use. Go through your bills and expenses and eliminate or reduce what you no longer use or need.

Strategically Use Credit Cards

Please understand that the following applies only to those people who are able to and pay their full bills before they are due so that they do not pay any finance charges or interest!

Most credit cards today have fees attached to them but also provide benefits. The most common benefit programs involve airline miles though there are cash back programs as well. Choose the program that provides the best benefits that you actually will use. Do not collect benefits that you are not going to use!

For me, I have made over 10 trips to Hawaii over the last 20 years and have yet to purchase any airfare. All of our flights, including children, we "purchased" with airline miles. That saved us over $750 a year! We pay a yearly fee of $80 for the cards but when you can save $750 a year paying the $80 is a no-brainer!

The grace period is another useful feature in that you can buy stuff today and not have to pay for it for as much as 6 weeks if you time it right. This only makes sense when you pay the balance in full every month. But you can use this grace period to your advantage and carefully schedule purchases so that the money is there when the bill shows up!

Be Responsible

Whether it is making more money or spending less, all of this will work only when you are responsible with your money. Use common sense when it comes to what you purchase and when you purchase it. Stay away from any kind of debt unless it is absolutely necessary.

For example, taking out a home mortgage you can afford might be a smart thing. Taking out a $10,000 loan for a 2 week vacation on Maui is not a good idea. You may have fun but when you get back you have to pay all that fun off plus interest.

Watch your money coming in as well as the money going out. Your goal should always be to have more coming in than you see going out. If it is the other way around, changes need to be made.

For more information on this and other topics, please visit our website at:

http://www.26ways.com